Despite the Plainness of the Day

Love Poems

David Ignatow

Despite the Plainness of the Day

Love Poems

David Ignatow

MILL HUNK BOOKS
Pittsburgh

Published by Mill Hunk Books, P.O. Box 71214, Pittsburgh, PA 15213
Manufactured in the United States of America

ISBN 0-9626023-0-2 cloth
ISBN 0-9626023-1-0 paperback

A number of these poems were first published in *Bluefish*, *Choice Magazine #9*, *Downtown #122*, *Long Pond Review*, *Men Talk Anthology* (1985), *Ninth Decade #1*, *The Ontario Review*, *Pacific Review*, *Paris Review*, *Poetry Magazine*, *Southern Humanities Review*, and *Williwaw*.

CONTENTS

Despite the Plainness of the Day

Love Poems

Despite the plainness of the day,
like all other days: the simple sun,
the ordinary wind, the usual trees
and the expected buildings, my cock
in you as I move back and forth
in happiness makes of the plain day
its own festive occasion.

Orgasm

It is the mind experiencing its pleasure,
its own flood, and as the flood recedes
leaves me calm and level as the Midwest plains,
fertile yet still. I rise from this calm
slowly, the way brush grows up silently
on the plains, where no eyes come upon it.
From brush, tall foliage under a permissive sky.
This is how I love my mind.

I walk with it, head held erect,
and I look at others thinking and hoping,
so that we may put our heads together
and hear each other's high, keen note
of pleasure in the self, life singing
to life, more beautiful
even than a single mind.

The Affection

The affection with which I approach you
is the expression of my affectionate self
which you have helped arouse by your presence
and so I offer you a kiss out of pleasure
in myself in thanks for your presence.
It is your face, no other at that moment
could have done the trick and so I look
into your eyes and you are pleased
that with my presence I have helped
to bring about this pleasure in yourself
at my regard. We are in love, each
with the other's power to induce
in us the happiness that comes
with self-regard.

Impermanence

The branches in the wind trace
your profile upon the air.
It disappears as quickly
as it has been drawn. Where
are you, I am left thinking.
Whose smile are you returning?

I am indifferent again I am obsessed by indifference Worried by
it Why indifference after I have discharged my stream of love
there you are breasts buttocks and belly lying beside me and I
converse with you on Dostoyevsky Tolstoy excitedly intelligently
you listen absorbed your eyes wander over my face with
detachment you too have discharged your love and can think and
see clearly again are we in love we are in conversation we have
enjoyed our sex as I talk I look at your body and do not
necessarily need to possess it look at your face it is lived
age is beginning to tell you look at mine age is beginning to tell
lines jowls we are middle-aged lovers who can discuss after a grand
orgasm together that was the body at work and now the mind the
self-regard which the mind stands for comes into play
our common interests must be stated we must find another way of
communicating fully besides through the body and we do it with
the mind we search for the fullness of communication and
understanding between us we are wary unsure eager to do well
uncertain of each other's mind and knowledge we will go on to
discover everything that can keep us together we talk stumble upon
the wrong phrase correct ourselves wait diffidently for the other to
speak react excitedly in response to convey interest identity with
agreement or a loving disagreement that will stimulate us to speak
even more rapidly and concretely we are opening paths to each
other this is so much more difficult than love and we are trying

Knowledge

Lying between her legs,
he was performing an obeisance.
It was his known self,
certainly not intended to create a child,
nor to make love the existence.
There would be transformations
of his bones and body in regal time,
time which was this thrusting
toward the sadness of climax
within an aperture of flesh,
as she who lay beneath him
heaved toward what they sought
in concert and that would bring them
to such pleasure as to obliterate,
at least for then,
the knowledge of their future life
beneath the soil.

See

It's not you in particular,
not your hair, nor breasts, nor belly,
thigh, voice, and subtly inviting movements.

It is not my asking and not your reply
and not my excitement
nor yours—this movement together
of nearly unendurable pleasure.

See from our bed,
now that we recline and rest,
how the wind lifts up
the unexceptionable waves
and sets them down.

The Puzzle

I came into the train and saw them standing together in a corner. One of the men was talking to the kid, as if it was his, you know, instructing the kid how to hold the lollipop, and giving the kid a hug like a father does, you know. The other guy was talking to the woman, like she was his wife. I heard them discussing dishes they received from some uncle. The other guy with the kid said something about the dishes, how he had placed them on the shelf. I was getting a bit confused. I could see the kid belonged to the woman, because the kid said "momma" once, when he wanted his mouth wiped. And the guy with the kid takes out his own handkerchief to wipe the kid's mouth and says to the woman, "We'll have to teach him to eat like a man." The other guy talking to the woman—the way these two looked at each other and the tones of their voices—I couldn't make out who was the father of the kid.

All the way to my station I was trying to make out who was the guy responsible. I studied their faces and the kid's, trying to make it out that way. The kid had brown eyes. One of the men had blue eyes, so I figured he was out. But then I remembered that brown eyes always came ahead of blue. I was going on like that all the way to my station. And once I saw one of the men, the one with the kid, listening to a conversation between the other one and the woman, and I thought from the manner in which they addressed him occasionally, with a smile, that he was a friend of the family, after all. But then, goddamn it, after the other had said something about being happy to get back from the trip, the woman holding his hand and smiling at him, I heard the guy with the kid say that he and Margaret—that's what he called the woman—had gotten in some new furniture while the other was away. That's the husband, I said to myself. The guy who said he got in the new furniture. The other is the friend. What the hell! Then I heard this one, the one who had been away, say to the woman, "Uncle told me to send him pictures of the kid, he wants to see his nephew." And the woman kept holding his hand and smiling at him. I was going nuts, really. Well, I had to get off at my station. It doesn't make any difference to me who was the father, maybe both were, the way it looked to me. I mean it doesn't make any difference to me how it happened, but it was puzzling. Suppose it was only one of the men, how in hell were you supposed to know?

In another dream I am embracing you floating above the ground,
my embrace partly intended to keep you from sailing off
into space. I am having difficulty keeping you down
finding myself being lifted, my heels beginning to leave
the ground, my toes clinging, but as they are about to take
off the ground itself begins to rise with me, to follow
our path upward. You and I sail off together, with earth
attached to my toes. We laugh, we are happy, free.

Your body is not mine
and so I look upon it
to contemplate a difference
that I study to accept
in just that difference
and yet because of it
makes a world for me
in that you're here
for the sake of difference
of which a world is made.

By the Nest of the Mother Bird

I love you in caves and meadows.
Flying, I love you.
In parks, streets, and alleys I love you.
By the bones of my mother,
by the clenched fist of my father.
By sunlight and by starlight,
by moonlight and by lamplight,
by phosphorous match
and by fire lit of dated newspapers,
by fire of dried twigs, in dark woods alone,
I love you
and by the nest of a mother bird,
nervous and angry at the sight of me,
I love you
I cannot remember anything without love of you.
I cannot remember living
without drawing breath.

VI

You spring from a fantasy
for charm, light, and beauty
I would give myself to
with outspread arms
and in your absence
fall.

Confusion is what I know best.
Look at me smiling at you,
making love to your eyes
to avoid further confusion
by offering myself. Are we
agreed as to its meaning?
Is the meaning between us
clear?

Meaningful is the conclusion
in which we two find ourselves,
for one touch of your hand
is the impress of our search
for its meaning. What are we
doing loving each other?

My love for you is a dark hall
through which I tap my way
along the walls for an exit
to an orchard under which
I may sit and speak
of my relationship to earth,
like that of the pear or the peach,
eaten for breakfast, filling
a need; desired in the daytime
and in the evening
and praised for its beauty
in the eye and in the mouth.

We shall love each other in bed, parlor, and kitchen
when we two meet as strangers in the guise of clerks,
lawyers, doctors, or what have you
that in no way resembles either you or us,
except that they have the bodies
like our own.

Peace to each of us.
Peace to the strangers.
Let them love each other
as we cannot now.

We write this to tell you
we are guilty
and cannot live without the guilt
and cannot live with it.

Keep Time Away

On some mornings she calls him up just as lunchtime begins, and croons into the phone, "Sweetheart. Yes, darling. Take it easy. Don't worry yourself, we'll manage," while she leans across the boss's desk, using his phone. He chews on a sandwich savagely, a glass of milk at his side. How he would like to fling her out of his office for using a business phone for such petty talk, but he needs her experience at the job. She croons a little longer, then hangs up gently so as not to give an impression of impatience at the other end. She is kind and good, fearful that a man can walk out on you, independent and haughty at having to be supported, suspecting contempt or belittlement from the other. She must be gentle with the last vestiges of love—that makes her arms go up and down at the gangstitcher, that makes her walk and talk buoyantly during lunch, that keeps her hair dyed brown and false teeth bright in her mouth, that makes her look toward the next day and say, "We'll manage."

And this boss, as she hangs up—he is chewing his sardine sandwich—says, with a full mouth, jaws clumping up and down, "Must you call up every day, and every day get calls back—from relatives too?" Poor man, he is anxious only for any business missed through her call, lacking the business that would let him eat in peace. As she thinks of a sharp answer, her face white and puffy, she restrains herself by clutching a handkerchief. She turns back into the shop to read the newspaper about the troubles of other people. The tears of her reddening eyes shine for a second in one last look at the boss. At her age, at fifty, to be told what to do and what not to do: to be denied or rebuked. At her age, when persons like herself have spent their energies to get some peace. For what else had all the fuss in her youth been but to assure her of that peace? At her age, still to be talked to like the worker she had been thirty years ago, except at that time she could understand it from an older person to a young girl. Still to face a young girl's havoc at her age, but without the strength or will to withstand it or to build upon it as youth does. Still, as if to stumble upon a rolling log upon a river, with no other safety or support but that rolling log. At her age of varicose veins, of great, burdensome breasts, of thick thighs and ponderous buttocks to be agile upon a log in the middle of a neverending rapid river. Her tears shine for a moment, dry up under the anger of the boss chewing sardines and sipping milk.

During lunch, all is quiet in the bindery. She sits beside the gangstitcher and reads with steel-rimmed glasses of what other people say and do that reminds her of her own circumstances. There is murder; there is insanity; sports to keep time away. Perversion, stag parties, robberies, and suicides. She reads and finds solace in that her case is not news enough to be printed: solace in knowing her predicament not yet that drastic.

Sound of a tiny bell brings the workers back from the corners of the bindery where they had sat eating, and the gangstitcher starts up again. With one last look at the boss through the open door of the office, she wonders if the day will go by without another word from him.

At home sits darling, brooding over his wife working to support him. How can she convince him that it is love and only love that keeps her here away from him?

Now

He's in class teaching
English literature and she
is approaching between the aisles
naked, her buttocks flowing,
her legs strutting
their pride in themselves.

No one else but he
sees her, which is exactly
as he wants it. She is
his private memory,
talking of Chaucer.

She seats herself,
crossing her legs,
brown pubic hair
forming a large dot
below her navel. She
looks at him and smiles,
the enigmatic kind,
as if to say, I'm here,
as you have asked of me.
Now are you at peace?

We are like two freight cars,
headed for each other cautiously
on the one track and about to couple
and take on freight for the nearest port.
Would you bother to question two
freight cars or watch them ride the rails
all day and night, the locomotive
whistling and hooting at each crossing,
like two lovers exchanging greetings
at the climax of their ecstasy
on their own roadbed.

It's so reassuring to show myself to you
naked when you are showing me your naked self
walking to and from bed. It's reassuring
of my secret self that has its nakedness
at heart and wishes to be known and loved
as I love all I am and will be ever.

What would life be without you?
It would be a life of imagining
as it has been with you. It is
a life of belief in my imagining,
as I have always believed,
as it sustains me, as it moves me
to act, as I acted in loving you
out of my imagining your self
and so I must continue
in the nature of my being
to love you still and always,
as I sustain myself in imagination
of your self, which sight supports me
to envision that I love as happily
as any man and more because of what
I have made come to life
through my imagining.

Neither One

A woman is pleading that she loves him and asking why he does not love her. His silence makes her believe he does not love her, and she says so in anguish. He can only look at her in silence. He does love her, but how can he say so under such pressure, as if it were something to confess, like a crime? He is resentful and filled with guilt at the same time, as if it were a crime to remain silent, as if it were a crime to keep his own counsel. He can love in silence, can't he? He can offer his presence. Why is that not enough for a person who is assured of love? It is the person who is not assured of love who insists otherwise and is unhappy, as she is by her pleading and unhappiness. And so the love he feels for her is filled with resentment that he does love such a person so unhappy with herself.

How did he come to choose her? Did he in fact choose? He can't answer, and he begins to distrust himself for having learned to love such a person, and now he begins to think that she does not love him, if she must insist that he speak to say he loves her. It may be that it is she who is not sure that she loves him, that she too is filled with resentment, real anger, and hostility and would prefer to hide it, overcome it in this inverse way of demanding to know about his love for her so that she can build a basis from which to reject him outright, and so he speaks to her—this time to advise her to quiet down, to take things easy, to return to her normal self, to make it possible for him to have a quiet, relaxed conversation with her, as in the past. And all the while he is inferring that this speech is coming from a concern for her out of love: a tactic to avoid saying outright what now has become unpleasant even to contemplate. Her face lights up, but he does not know exactly what suddenly she seems to have realized about him and about herself—about him that he is succumbing to her onslaught? But conversely making it difficult for her, since it is anger more than love—or is it love turned to anger that is at the root of her campaign to make him speak? Her voice lowers, grows relaxed. It speaks more calmly, and they are back to where they were before her sudden anxiety. They talk about bills and the children and the repairs for the house and the need for a new car. Everything is back to normal, and neither one is satisfied.

Does my blood need a motive
to travel the length of my body,
picking up waste, discharging waste,
taking on health? Do I need
to explain why loving you
is important and why leaving
is equally so, as when my blood
slows, meeting impediments; halts
and dies? You and I have met
to transact some business
between us and my delight
is in measure with our success
and my warmth toward you.
What other meaning can I find
for us, if there be meaning here
as when stars collapse
and new ones are born
out of the same matter?

I Dream I Hurl a Spear

I dream I hurl a spear into the body of my love.
I am brutal, but the spear begins to glow along its shaft
and transfixes me. I stand covered in its radiance,
unable to move, magnetized toward the spear that I reach
out to touch and then grasp and stroke and carry myself
forward along its length until I have touched the body
of my love itself at the point where the spear has entered.
I sob, I shake in convulsions, and the body of my love
bends forward to comfort me as I support myself against
it in a paroxysm of leaving my body.

Here I am in a room with a woman dressed only in her panties,
her rounded, firm breasts bobbing with each energetic
movement toward things she is attached to or finds need
to be done, such as packing, wiping away dust. I am glancing
up from time to time from my book of essays, to observe her
but with no impulse to stand up to move toward her. It's
as if desire were spent or inappropriate or merely romantic
in a context of daily occupations, such as packing, cleaning,
and reading from a book of essays on the nature of the poet,
the thinker, the maker.

The World

The world opens as you receive me
in the warmth and wet of my first birth,
born to be a joy to myself and to you.
I am alive to tell it
for the truth that is its own joy
as I live in two worlds at once,
yours in which I move ecstatically
and that which is the words for it.

I am alive forever, knowing of the happiness
of those yet to be, and so I feel no fear,
vanished in you. I am my own creator
ever to be and never to deny it
in the grave.

Midnight II

In place of you
the moon is a presence
in my room I must turn
my back on to sleep
in the dark.

It's not you I miss
but the weave of thought
around your presence
with which to clothe
the bareness of my life—
a cloth of the colors
of the days and nights
we spent together.

He stops his wife in the street
and looks into her bakery bag
for the breakfast delicacies.
The day is Sunday and temperate,
the sun mild. She wears shorts.
Her face is unremarkable,
with a kind of petulant mouth.
In the bag he finds what he is
looking for. They talk together
quickly and lightly and then he
continues up the street and she
resumes her way to the apartment.
Swinging his arms and legs wide,
he walks chipper: his wife has
shapely thighs.

Summer

Sideways to the sea we walked,
reviewing the soda stands, the shooting galleries,
pavilion-sitters to whom wind was air.
We walked so that we tired ourselves
of our freedom, beaten by wind. How it roared.
It became monotonous. We looked at each other
and saw enslavement, sea to shore.

We suggested hot dogs. And after swallowing
soda water, we strolled the park where trees
held off the crazy wind. And in the park
the pathways were the shore,
our feet the restless waves.
Now in the distance we heard the subway
roar a freedom of dark tunnels.

It was a lovely ride,
with nothing to say to one another.
At home, the newspaper spread out upon the couch
told us of freedoms won or gone or to come,
fresh fruit stinging our mouths.
At our window, the sun sank in choleric rage.

Bare to the waist, I defied the elements,
and in your slip you were Diana of the hunt.
You did not move, reading your side of the news,
which was to wait for your pursuer
to come so close that you could whirl.
Each would root the other to the spot,
freed of ourselves.

It is peculiar that you should love me;
I see myself as frog or toad.
Calmly I turn away.

There you go, pleading with me,
your voice strained and hoarse,
angry. Are you frog or toad too?

I smile and kiss your cheek,
rest an arm across your shoulder.

Wrong

Why do I resent you?
Because you are not my mother.
Where are you when I need you?
But you are a person in your own right,
as I am made to feel about myself,
which I resent, detached from the harbor
in which I anchored or sailed safely,
the two arms of her shore embracing me
from the toppling sea.

What must I do to become a person as you—
forget you in your absence,
as you forget me? Or, as you say,
concentrate on what is before me
and enjoy? But I am without love
as I know it and now I must love
this absence as myself, as you love
yourself in my absence—as I cannot
because I miss my mother
and am wrong.

Your face before me
in the room as I speak
with another
starts a silence
in my mind of worship
of your beauty.

We catch each other staring.
You then turn away
to divert yourself
with someone at your side.
I resume with another,
the sensation
of having made love
to you in the look
we two exchanged.

I like how your belly
forms a half moon
under your skirt.

I think of the fullness
of love. My hand travels
over it gently, the peace
in me of fulfillment.

I'm a Machine

I'm a machine that needs to be told I'm not a machine. Who will take my perfect hand and kiss my perfect lips to deny my existence as a machine? Who will love me for myself to make me feel myself an even greater machine, one that flies at the touch of a hand or a kiss on its synthetic lips, two machines entering into each other's gears, cylinders, and sprockets?

What kind of machine are you then that cannot love my machine? What other machine are you looking for? Is there a happiness programmed in your system as it is in mine but requires a particular kind for which I am not programmed? I would like to know so that I could content myself with my limits in order that I may function smoothly once again as in the past, then when I was in love with my efficiency and loved myself and needed no one else, but then I became elated by my performance toward myself and sought out another with whom to share my excellence, so much there was of it that it had spread to others and touched you.

Who am I to be loved,
subject to error;
which is to say I should love
in return those who resemble me
none of whom please me entirely
but offer opportunity
for complaints.

How am I qualified to be loved,
criticizing those who love me
whom I love in return,
with no recourse
than to love because
I am human and must love
to be human.

The Sea Is My Place

You have brought me to an opening to the sea for each to sail in separate ships that will meet only as the waves bring us together. It's as you wish, I an island man led by your beauty to this shore, your hair in the wind like a wave.

I was a rooted man, my feet trailing beneath the surface for the springs of earth. I adventured where I stood, I envisioned you and it was as in a vision that you led me here where I stand beside you, feeling myself without a place, now that you will sail without me, but here is where I was brought to know myself from earth and on this trackless sea make myself a shifting place.

Are dreams as real as roots? Why then do I fear and study you, seeking for the knowledge in which you leave? Is the sea a place? Are you a place? And if that is the knowledge in which you leave, what moves within me, flowing me outward with the force of fear? And if it is fear then it is I and I am place, too, taking myself with me upon the waves.

I ask you to answer about yourself as you look out to sea, as your smile draws me with the force of fear. I place my hand upon your face and I know the sea is my place.

Fall

No, no, no, the leaves are saying, thrashing about in the wind.
We don't want to go; we don't want to be parted from our branch.
We love it here, even as we brown with age. Love must be forever,
or it is not love, and the leaves fling themselves to and fro in
the wind. The dark comes and no longer can the leaves be seen,
though they can be heard thrashing to and fro and against each other.

The Wound

This longing to be healed in you
each night in bed without you
is a struggle to breathe.

Reality is the other person.
We are all imagination
on whom the other intrudes
to give us pain and sorrow
of our unfulfillment
in the other.

The love we had for one another is somewhere
missing, unhappy with ourselves
and sad for one another, as if
we have consigned each other to oblivion.

I love you from a distance,
I hear your voice behind a wall
calling me to find a path around,
if but to show myself
at least alive, if not in love
but willing to be seen with you.

Let others think what they may,
we'll have the mask
that fits the face of grief,
at risk among others.

Without sexual attraction, there is
the brutal movement of the sea.
The face peers out of its skeletal frame
and hands reach like bone.

Without love, the streets
are hollow sounding
with wooden, hurried steps,
voices like caverns of death.
We pass each other as trains do,
whistling screams.

The Life

To rest in love as a water bug rests on the surface, swinging to and fro with the gentle rhythm of the tide, then lightly dashing across the surface to catch his yet tinier victim.

What would I dash over the surface for? To catch at my prey, the poem that like the victim of the water bug would affirm my life: to rest in love as on a water bed, with all my frame snugly fitting, and every which way I turn the surface holding me closely. I'd lose my sense of self in this watery support, the self of hip and thigh, my head, too, afloat. Let this be the life of love.

About the Author

David Ignatow has won a number of awards for his poetry—the Bollingen Prize in 1977, and, earlier, two Guggenheim fellowships, the Wallace Stevens fellowship from Yale University, the Rockefeller Foundation fellowship, the Shelley Memorial and the National Institute of Arts and Letters awards. He was poet-in-residence at Walt Whitman's birthplace in 1987. He is president emeritus of the Poetry Society of America.

Since 1964 Ignatow has taught at the New School for Social Research, the University of Kentucky, the University of Kansas, Vassar College, York College of the City University of New York, and New York University. He is now adjunct senior lecturer at Columbia University. He was an editor for *The American Poetry Review*, *Chelsea Magazine*, *The Nation*, *The Beloit Poetry Journal*, and *Analytic*. He is the author of fourteen books of poetry and three prose books. He lives in East Hampton, Long Island.

Mill Hunk Books are published by Peter Oresick and Anthony Petrosky for Piece of the Hunk Publishers, Inc., a non-profit, working class cultural organization in Pittsburgh, Pennsylvania.

Despite the Plainness of the Day was edited by Peter Oresick and Anthony Petrosky and copyedited by Kathy McLaughlin.